THE
HAIKU
TAO TE CHING

THE HAIKU TAO TE CHING

Wisdom of the Tao for People in a Hurry

Tom F. Lang

authorHOUSE®

AuthorHouse™
1663 Liberty Drive
Bloomington, IN 47403
www.authorhouse.com
Phone: 1-800-839-8640

First published by AuthorHouse   08/04/2011

ISBN: 978-1-4634-4865-3 (sc)
ISBN: 978-1-4634-4864-6 (ebk)

Library of Congress Control Number: 2011913999

Printed in the United States of America

Introduction

The Tao Te Ching, believed to be written by Lao Tzu in about 700 B.C.E., is one of the most widely published books in the world, second only to the Holy Bible. But the lessons to be learned from Lao Tzu's teachings are still relevant today.

The Tao is often referred to as The Nameless because neither it nor its principles can ever be adequately expressed in words. It is sometimes referred to as The Way. It has no shape or form, is simultaneously perfectly still and constantly moving, is both larger than the largest thing and smaller than the smallest. It describes a universe bounded by an infinitely large omnipotent, omniscient intelligence, which lies behind everything.

Haiku is a major form of Japanese verse. A Haiku, developed in the 17th century by Zen monks, expresses a single feeling or impression and contains three unrhymed lines usually consisting of five, seven, and five syllables, respectively.

It is impossible to condense all of knowledge of the Tao Te Ching into a verse of 3 lines, 17 syllables for each of its 81 chapters. But by studying a number of the translations of this ancient document, together with other related writings, I have attempted to, at least, instill the spirit of this work into Haiku verse. I hope that this small book can provide a welcome thought when a spiritual lift is desired, as well as a quick, anytime reminder of the wisdom contained in this ancient Chinese text.

Tom F. Lang

1

Tao, the path of truth,

    its mystery unchanging,

        cannot be described.

2

Opposites abound;

being and nonbeing form.

All are one with Tao.

3

Living life simply

    and pursuing not status

        leads to contentment.

4

The Tao has no form.

It harmonizing all things;

unites them as one.

5

Quiet and ceaseless,

    and acting not from impulse,

      is the way of Tao.

6

Inexhaustible,

    it gives birth to endless worlds.

    Spirit immortal.

7

The people of Tao

    transcend life; find fullfilment

        through loving service.

8

When you are content

and don't compare and compete,

all will respect you.

9

Excess cannot last.

Flaunting wealth invites trouble.

It is not the Way.

10

Be detached from things,

   not wishing to possess them.

   And give of yourself.

11

Wheel, cup or window;

    it is the hollow center

        that makes them useful.

12

Let go of excess.

Precious things lead one astray.

Seek inner wisdom.

13

Favor and disgrace

    are equally to be feared.

        Both may be fleeting.

14

The Tao is formless,

> the image of nothingness.

> > Yet it forms all things.

15

He who follows Tao

   will not be full of himself,

      but will go unseen.

16

Throughout all nature,

    see how living things flourish

    and renew themselves.

17

The Sage dares to trust.

    We will never be trusted

        if we never trust.

18

If the Tao is lost,

    one meets darkness and turmoil,

        and much confusion.

19

Without selfishness

    and artful contrivances,

        there would be no thieves.

20

Simplify your life.

Ignore the competition;

be detached and still.

21

Within the great Tao

  are found principles of truth;

   the lessons of life.

22

The Sage sees Oneness

  as a model for the world

    and becomes a guide.

23

Become one with Tao

    by affirming gentleness.

        Force cannot sustain.

24

One who flaunts himself,

who insists that he is right,

impedes his own growth.

25

The Sage regards Tao

as the Mother of all things

in the Universe.

26

The Sage follows Tao.

Though he may have a mansion,

his life is simple.

27

The Sage helps others

and uses all things wisely.

Nothing is wasted.

28

As a Tao person,

    you move with greater power,

        drawing from the Source.

29

The world is changing.

Those who would make it conform

will never succeed.

30

To conquer by force

will bring only resistance.

It will not endure.

31

In winning a war

do not rejoice. There is no

delight in killing.

32

You need do nothing.

The Tao is omnipresent;

perfect harmony.

33

To know men is wise;

    to know oneself is insight.

        The Sage knows himself.

34

Tao is pervasive.

It requires nothing, and yet

all depend on it.

35

Hold fast to the Tao.

Happiness, harmony, peace,

and joy will follow.

36

When one first breathes in,

it follows exhalation.

This is natural.

37

Desires fall away

　　revealing one's true nature

　　　　when one lives simply.

38

The highest virtue

is to give without constraint.

Make this your nature.

39

All things will decay.

Were it not for the great Tao,

There would be no life.

40

Mother of all things,

    the Tao moves by returning

        in endless cycles.

41

The Tao is hidden,

    but skilled at imparting things

        to those who listen.

42

Tao created one;

    one became two; two caused three;

      three produced legion.

43

That which is softest

    goes where there is no crevice

    and gently prevails.

44

When you have enough,

be content with what you have.

Know sufficiency.

45

To follow the Tao

  in wisdom and stillness brings

   order to the world.

46

Never wanting more,

abiding in contentment,

the Sage finds his bliss.

47

By seeking within

　　the Sage knows; going nowhere,

　　　　he finds completion.

48

The practice of Tao

creates simplification.

One needs do nothing.

49

The Sage reaches out,

    regarding all living things

      as one family.

50

The Sage contributes,

   not thinking of his actions.

      They flow from his core.

51

The Tao produces

    all things; brings them to full growth,

        but does not claim them.

52

Stay with the great Tao

and the essence of your life

will never be lost.

53

The highest wisdom

    is to walk the path of Tao,

        yet many digress.

54

Tao cannot be lost.

Cultivated, it will thrive

and grow without end.

55

Harmony knows peace.

That which is against the Tao

will wither away.

56

Talkers do not know.

Silence is your evidence

of inner knowing.

57

The master of Tao

    makes few rules and restrictions;

      does not give orders.

58

If laws are subdued,

    people are mostly happy.

        Crossed, they are sullen.

59

Naught surpasses thrift.

Return to the simple life.

There's nothing better.

60

When living the Tao,

energy is not repressed,

but redirected.

61

Centered in the Tao,

   if a great country lowers

      itself, it wins trust.

62

Tao supports all things;

    a treasure for the worthy,

        a path for the lost.

63

Hold the same regard

for the few and the many.

Show kindness to all.

64

The Sage spoils nothing,

    contrives or clings to nothing,

        thus loses nothing.

65

He who leads others

    with harmony and wisdom

      will benefit much.

66

The Sage guides people.

He serves with humility

and follows behind.

67

Three things you should be:

simple, kind, compassionate.

That is indeed great.

68

A good warrior

    does not win by challenging.

    He is not hostile.

69

When conflict happens,

a great treasure, peace, is gone.

Only grief will win.

70

The Tao is easy

to know; to facilitate.

Yet so few practice.

71

We cease to be sick

when we are sick of sickness.

This is the secret.

72

Respect where you dwell.

Love your life and livelihood,

thus you enjoy life.

73

The Sage does not strive,

    does not contend, is gentle.

        Gentleness brings peace.

74

Those who take the place

of a skilled carver often

risk cutting their hands.

75

When they are oppressed,

    people will lose their spirit.

        Allow them freedom.

76

Softness, suppleness,

flexibility prevail.

Rigid, hard will break.

77

The nature of Tao

    takes from what is excessive

        and gives it to lack.

78

Water is yielding.

Yet for dissolving hardness
naught can surpass it.

79

Work for agreement.

Wise people seek solutions;

ignorant cast blame.

80

Live life in balance.

Delight in life's rituals

and meaningful work.

81

Those skilled in the Tao

do not dispute it. They give,

yet their needs are met.

Bibliography

CLEARY, Thomas
     The Essential Tao
DREHER, Diane
     The Tao of Inner Peace;
     The Tao of Personal Leadership
DYER, Dr. Wayne W. Dyer
     Change Your Thoughts, Change Your Life
GIBBS, Tam C.
     "My Words Are Very Easy To Understand."
JOHANSON, Greg and KURTZ, Ron
     Grace Unfolding
LEGGE, James
     The Texts of Taoism
NI, Hua-Ching
     The Complete Works of Lao Tzu

Fascinated by the Haiku art form, and a long-time student of the Tao, the author became intrigued by the idea of blending the two. This book is the culmination of his efforts.

With this new interpretation of the Tao Te Ching, the author utilizes the brevity of Haiku to render this ancient classic into what he believes to be a collection of 81 succinct nuggets of Eastern wisdom.